Meat-eating Plants

by Kelly Gaffney

a Capstone company — publishers for children

Engage Literacy is published in the UK by Raintree.
Raintree is an imprint of Capstone Global Library Limited, a company incorporated in England and Wales
having its registered office at 264 Banbury Road, Oxford, OX2 7DY – Registered company number: 6695582

www.raintree.co.uk

Editorial credits
Jennifer Huston, editor; Richard Parker, designer; Pam Mitsakos, media researcher; Katy LaVigne, production specialist

Image credits
Getty Images: David Cavagnaro, 21, Ed Reschke, 17; Minden Pictures: Barry Mansell/NPL, 7, Michel Rauch/Biosphoto,
5, Nick Garbutt/NPL, 15; Shutterstock: Aggie 11, back cover, aLittleSilhouetto, 9, antishock, design elements, Barbara
Brockhauser, 1, 11, Cathy Keifer, cover top left, ChameleonsEye, 22, Egon Zitter, cover top right, Jaime Pharr, 19,
Kuttelvaserova Stuchelova, 10, Leah-Anne Thompson, 8, Marco Uliana, cover bottom middle, Matthijs Wetterauw, 12,
ordinary man, cover background, scaners3d, 13, 23

Glossary
argus, (sunlight), BlueRingMedia, (nutrient), GraphicsRF, (nectar), Lorelyn Medina, (swamp), (tube), Pushkin, (rainwater),
Spreadthesign, (insect)

10 9 8 7 6 5 4 3 2 1
Printed and bound in China.

Meat-eating Plants

ISBN: 9781474739283

Contents

Plants that eat meat

Plants are found all over the world.
They come in many different shapes
and sizes.
Some plants are huge, while others
are tiny.

Plants need *sunlight* to make food.
They also need *nutrients* from the soil
around them.
Nutrients are things that people, animals
and plants need to be strong and healthy.

There is one very strange group
of plants that eats meat.
Meat-eating plants feed
on all sorts of *insects*.
Some even eat small frogs and mice.

Where do meat-eating plants grow?

Meat-eating plants can grow
in places where the soil isn't very good.
Most grow in wet, soggy areas,
like *swamps*.
Others grow in rocky areas.

Meat-eating plants get the nutrients
they need from the things they eat.
Even though these plants eat insects
and small animals, they still need
sunlight and water to live.

Meat-eating plants have many
interesting ways of catching their food.
Some of them move quickly to trap insects.
Others don't move at all!

The Venus flytrap

One well-known plant that eats meat
is the Venus flytrap.
It uses something called
a "snap trap" to catch insects.

The snap trap is made of two leaves
with very thin hairs between them.

If an insect walks across the plant,
it might touch these hairs.
When the hairs are touched,
the two leaves snap shut.

When the leaves of the Venus flytrap
snap shut, the insect becomes trapped.
The harder the insect tries to get out,
the more the leaves push together.

Next, the plant starts to break down
the insect and use it for food.
This takes about two weeks.
The leaves stay closed during this time.

The sundew plant

Another meat-eating plant
is the sundew plant.

The sundew plant has leaves that are
covered with long, thin hairs.

The ends of these hairs are very sticky. When an insect lands on the sticky hairs, it gets stuck.

The more the insect tries to get away, the more difficult it becomes to move. When the insect dies, the plant's leaves wrap around the insect.

The dead insect slowly breaks down into little pieces. Then the plant uses it for food.

Pitcher plants

There is another group of meat-eating plants called pitcher plants.
Pitcher plants come in different shapes and sizes.
They don't move at all.

Pitcher plants have tall leaves that look like jugs or long *tubes*.
Rainwater collects at the bottom of these leaves.

Some pitcher plants
have pretty flowers
and give off
a sweet smell
that insects like.
But when an insect
goes into one
of the pitcher
plant's tubes,
it gets trapped.
It's very hard
for an insect
to get out once it
has fallen into
a pitcher plant.

Pitcher plants have different ways
of trapping insects.
Some insects fall straight into the water
from the top of the pitcher plant.
Others climb into the pitcher plant's tube
looking for food.
Once an insect is inside the pitcher
plant, it can't get out.
The sides of the tube are very slippery.
They have sharp hairs that point down.
An insect may try to get out,
but it soon falls down into the water.

Some insects cannot swim.
Others can't climb out of the tube.
All of these things help the pitcher plant
to catch insects.

Insects that are trapped
in the pitcher plant will die.
After they die, they are used as food
by the pitcher plant.

The cobra lily

The cobra lily is another interesting
meat-eating plant.
It has tall leaves that make a tube,
like other pitcher plants.
But the top of the cobra lily
curls up and around.

The cobra lily feeds on small insects.
It catches insects by making sweet *nectar*.
Insects eat nectar.
When an insect lands on the top
of a cobra lily, it smells the nectar
inside the plant.
The insect follows the smell.

It then goes in through an opening
near the top of the plant.
Once it is inside the plant,
the insect starts eating the nectar.
The insect goes farther and farther
into the plant as it eats the nectar.

When the insect has finished eating,
it tries to find its way out.
The insect searches for the small opening
near the top of the plant.
But the opening is hidden
in the darkness.

The insect flies around
inside the plant until it dies.
Once the insect is dead,
the cobra lily uses it for food.

There are many different kinds of meat-eating plants.

Most eat insects, but some eat frogs, mice and even small birds!

Some meat-eating plants move quickly to trap their food.

Others don't need to move at all.

Meat-eating plants are very strange, but they are very interesting, too.

Picture glossary

insect

sunlight

nectar

swamp

nutrient

tube

rainwater